the
# natural
# garden

# the
# natural
# garden

common
sense lore
passed down
through
generations

## Rosamond Richardson

with photographs by Michelle Garrett

Kyle Cathie Limited

First published in Great Britain in 2001 by
Kyle Cathie Limited
122 Arlington Road, London NW1 7HP

ISBN 1 85626 415 7

**The material in this book is taken mostly from COUNTRY WISDOM by Rosamond Richardson, published in 1997**

A CIP catalogue record for this title is available from the British Library

Production by Lorraine Baird & Sha Huxtable
Colour reproduction by ChromaGraphics, Singapore
Printed and bound in Italy by Printer Trento S. r. l.

**Photography credits: Pages 1, 2/3, 35, 43 Clay Perry; Pages 9, 54, 56/57 GPL/Clive Boursnell; Page 18; Ecoscene/David Wootton; Page 24, 46 Fran Yorke; Page 28 GPL/Jane Legate; Page 50/1 GPL/John Miller; Page 54 GPL/J.S Sira; Pages 55, 59, 67 GPL/John Glover; Page 40, Holt/Nigel Catlin; Page 63, Timothy Whidborne; Page 69, Holt/Bob Gibbons; Page 70, GPL/Jerry Pavia; Page 72 Holt/Willem Harinck; Page 22 (right) GPL/Ron Sutherland; Page 23 (left) GPL/Tim Spence; Page 23 (right) GPL/Nigel Francis; Page 27 GPL/Tim McMillan; Page 49 Sally Maltby**

# CONTENTS

Introduction  6

Weather Lore  10

Planting Wisdom  18

Soil & Compost  24

Companion Planting  36

Good Plants and Garden Flower Lore  48

Herbal Wisdom  60

Bees & Butterflies  74

Garden Pests  76

Index  80

# INTRODUCTION

*The gardener half artist must depend*
*On that slight chance, that touch beyond control*
*Which all his paper planning will transcend;*
*He knows the means but cannot rule his end;*
*He makes the body: who supplies the soul?*

*Vita Sackville West: 'The Garden'*

From earliest civilisation mankind has engaged in the engrossing activity of cultivating a small enclosed piece of ground called a garden: a personal paradise – 'a green thought in a green shade' – to fulfil practical or aesthetic needs, or both. From sacred groves and a vision of an archetypal Eden have evolved flower and fruit gardens, kitchen gardens, rose gardens, pleasure gardens and landscape gardens. As he planted and toiled, knowing success and failure, a vast tradition of gardening wisdom both oral and written began to grow. It is immense, international and universal.

I have gleaned some of this traditional wisdom by talking with many gardeners who have contributed their commonsense experience to this book. Other pieces I picked up in days of childhood from my mother's gardener, Mr Williams, who became my personal archetype. He worked for us for many years, and our garden was to me the magical place of childhood. I loved to trail around after him, watch what he did and pester him with questions. His way of speaking and turn of phrase are lodged in my memory. He seemed very old indeed to me then, a tall stooping man who always wore a cap and an old tweed jacket. He was forever dropping wise remarks about the wind or the weather, the phases of the moon or which plants to put next to

**A garden can be a personal paradise for cultivating flowers, fruits and vegetables.**

7

which, all of which he had learned from his grandfather. Most of it went over my head then, but as I started to tend a garden myself much of it resurfaced, and it appears here in its inherited version.

Making a selection of the country wisdom of the garden is a well-nigh impossible task. Books enough to fill libraries have been written all over the world and throughout the ages on the fascinating areas of divining weather, planting at the correct phase of the moon, enriching the soil with compost, companion planting, the work of bees and butterflies, the curse of insect pests, and the microlife of a garden. Likewise, the folklore of flowers and trees, steeped as it is in a fascinating mixture of science and superstition, is impressive in its immensity. A few pages can claim only to give a taste of this universal practical wisdom with its delicate touches of fantasy.

**Traditional gardening wisdom is vast and international, touching on both the practical and the whimsical.**

# WEATHER LORE

*'Those that are weather wise*
*Are rarely otherwise'*

Although much traditional weather lore is unsubstantiated, it still prevails and in many cases meteorological science has not come up with anything better. The roots of weather lore lie in early religion. Its first exponents were priests or wise men who decided the all-important dates of sowing or harvest. Fertility of the crops, on which survival depended, meant the interpreting aright of weather signs.

## Fine Weather

Year after year I remember Mr Williams saying the weather would be fine if swallows, martins or skylarks fly high, and he never tired of repeating 'Red sky at night, shepherd's delight.' A friend who lives in northern California quotes this version:

*Red sky at night*
*Shepherd's (Sailor's) delight*

Common as this saying is in its various forms, it is not always trustworthy although the next part of it, just as widespread:

*Red sky at morning*
*Shepherd's (Sailor's) warning*

is found in various forms throughout the world and reflects a scientific reality, of the scattering of light rays linked to thermal stratification or the formation of atmospheric currents. It is a generally accepted as a reliable piece of weather lore.

**'Red sky at night, shepherd's delight' is a portent of fine weather.**

# CLOUDS AND WIND

Clouds may indicate weather changes: 'mackerel sky, twelve hours dry'. My neighbour used to call it a 'cruddly' sky: in meteorological terms this sky, dappled with small white fleecy clouds, is a cirrocumulus formation marking the end of unsettled weather. Looking at the movement of upper layers of clouds can tell you if a change of weather is imminent, if their direction is very different from the winds blowing clouds below. A Moroccan woman told me a famous legend that locusts know where it will rain in the Sahara. In actual fact swarms fly downwind until they meet an area of convergent winds, where rain is most likely.

Virgil said that 'Rain and wind increase after a thunderclap', and this appears to be borne out as an accurate observation throughout the centuries. The Zuni Indians of New Mexico had a saying that 'If the first thunder is from the east, winter is over', also grounded in generations of experience and found to be true. But probably the best guide to weather prediction, grounded in careful observation by men and women close to the cycles of nature, is in the wind: Francis Bacon said that 'Every wind has its weather', a belief shared by many cultures from the Ancient Greeks to the American Indians. 'Do business with men when the wind in the north-west, goes an old saying from the north of England.

**Looking at the movement of clouds can tell you if a change of weather is imminent.**

**Owls hoot more at night and cocks crow more frequently, when there is rain about.**

# RAIN

Many persistent country sayings of weather lore are not grounded in science, but nor
have they been disproved. If ants retreat into their burrows rain will not be far behind.
If a candle will not light easily, it means rain; a wavering flame means windy weather is
on the way. If the down flies off dandelions, coltsfoot or thistles when there is no
wind, it is a sign of rain. 'Rain from the east, two wet days at least' may be mere
observations, but they may contain some veracity. An Irish musician told me that the
call of a curlew predicts a downpour, and that horses get restless and shake their
heads just before rain. One of the most prevalent beliefs is that 'it will rain if cattle lie
down in the fields'. Possibly cattle have learnt, and passed on through their genes as an

adaptive process, to bag a dry spot before it is too late. The most that can be said is that animals do indeed behave in particular ways under certain meteorological conditions, and so can be said to provide a forecast of kinds. Bees fly home if bad weather is coming, many insects hatch in the humid weather before a storm, and swallows fly low to catch them. Owls hoot more at night, and cocks crow more frequently, when there is rain about.

My German friend Inge's grandfather worked on the land all his life. He swore that he could predict rain by his corns and rheumatism. Widespread as this lore is, there is no evidence to prove the connection, Men, like plants and animals, react quickly to climate, but other factors such as diet, temperament and anxiety levels preclude generalisations.

An old lady from deepest Herefordshire told me that in her experience beetles always come out of their haunts before rain, and worms too, presumably to escape drowning; whereas 'Fine weather next day if bats or beetles fly late in the evening' is a common country saying in East Anglia. My friends from Oregon mentioned trees such as poplar and silver maple turning up their leaves when it starts to rain, an observation well-known in Europe also. Scientists now know that plants react quickly to their environment and their survival depends on the genetic transmission of safety responses, so they can be read as consistent weather indicators.

I was brought up with the dictum from my American mother 'rain before seven, dry before eleven', and learned early to distinguish a rain cloud – the cumulus cloud:

> *A round-topped cloud with a flattened base*
> *Carries rainfall in its face*

Many people including myself take a rain check on St. Swithin's Day (July 15th), for 'if it do rain, for forty days it will remain'. This piece of lore has entered commonplace wisdom, based on long-term observations and passed on down through generations.

Science has not been able to either prove or disprove it, nor to replace it with anything superior. Likewise with this well-known piece of country weather lore which Wilf, my beekeeper neighbour, used to come out with every year:

*If the oak's before the ash*
*There will only be a splash*
*If the ash before the oak*
*Then we're sure to get a soak*

# COLD WEATHER

When I was a child my best friend's grandfather always used to say 'If the cat turns her back on the fire there will be frost'. My old neighbour Wilf, in his best Essex dialect, used to say: 'An east wind is a lazy one, it will go through you before it goes round you.' These signs were immutable: If nuts or berries hang on the branches after leaf fall, it means a hard winter ahead : 'Many haws, many sloes, many cold toes'. And 'When the oak wears his leaves in October you can expect a hard winter.'

*Holly berries shining red*
*Mean a long winter, 'tis said.*

There is always one fine week in February in England, or later if winter is late; but beware the 'blackthorn hatch'. This warm weather brings the sloe into blossom, but spring is not just around the corner: it is immediately followed by a patch of very severe weather. Ever since Wilf, sadly now departed, told me this, I have observed it happen unfailingly each year.

We all know that 'If March comes in like a lion, it goes out like a lamb' and vice versa. And 'cast not a clout till May be out' because 'In the middle of May comes the tail of winter', according to the wise.

# THE MOON

The moon features large in weather lore, in spite of the absence of scientific explanation. The nearest is the 'ring around the moon', a white halo sometimes tinged with red, formed by refraction through ice crystals in the clouds and is often seen when rain is approaching. It is not however infallible. A woman from Oregon told of her mother's dictum that a ring a round the moon means rain next day – a well-known saying around the world.

> *If the moon shows like a silver shield*
> *You needn't be afraid to reap your field;*
> *But if she rises haloed round,*
> *Soon we'll tread on deluged ground*

**The moon is an enduring focus of weather lore.**

Some country folk say that a new moon brings a change in the weather; that sharp horns means windy weather, and the full moon clears the sky and brings good weather.

*The moon on its back*
*Holds rain in its lap*

Emanuele, living in rural France near Vaugines, has noted that when the weather turns bad at the start of the new moon, it will stay bad for the whole lunar cycle. In her experience, she says, it seems to be true.

# PLANTING WISDOM

The phases of the moon are closely associated with fertility, and their importance in planting lore occurs so often all over the world that it is hard to dismiss them as superstition. Traditional wisdom has it that the moment you put a seed into the ground is of utmost importance for its success: root crops should be planted when the moon is waning, while a new moon is auspicious for those above ground so that the waxing moon influences them. I am convinced that there is something in this, so is an Indian friend who has the greenest fingers of anyone I know.

**Cornseed should be planted on a waxing moon.**

# PLANTING WISDOM

'Sow corn when the moon is waxing, never when it is waning' goes an English saying. The exception is with watery plants like marrows, cucumbers and courgettes which are best set at full moon. A gardener in Shropshire who had worked the land all his life quoted this:

*Cut all things or gather, the moon in the wane,*
*But sow in increasing, or give it its bane.*

From a homestead on the Welsh borders, 'Set peas and beans at the wane of the moon, and onions, carrots and parsnips at the change.' The mother of an Indian friend who lives in Jaipur told me that onions are much larger and better nourished if set during the wane. Plant potatoes with a rising tide so they grow with it, and set or sow all kind of pulse with the Moon in Cancer.

A Dutch friend's grandmother has a saying, 'Trees are not to be grafted the Moon waning, or not to be seen'.

## The Seasons

My mother's gardener used to say:

*Drunk or sober,*
*Sow wheat in October*

and

*Who in January sows oats,*
*Gets gold and groats*

He would always set garlic and broad beans on the shortest day, advice I successfully followed in the days when I had a vegetable patch. Sow onions, he said, on St Gregory's Day (12th March) for a good crop. To do well, shallots should be sown on December 21st along with the garlic and pulled on the longest (June 21st). Other pearls of wisdom included sowing potatoes when the yellow wagtail arrives in spring, usually March.

## The weather and the time of day

Thomas Hyll, in his mid-16th-century *The Sowing and Care of Seedlings*, tells us that 'Seed must be sown on a mild, clear day and not when a north wind is blowing, nor the day verie cold, for in such seasons and dayes (as all the skilful report) the earth as then timorous and fast shut, hardly receyueth and nourisheth the seedes committed to it.'

Sometimes however country lore contradicts itself – hedging its bets perhaps: 'Sow dry and set in the wet'. Yet: 'sow beans in the mud and they'll grow like a wood'. And 'sow in a slop, 'twill be heavy at top.' If you can squeeze a handful of soil together and it sticks, it is too wet to plant. Sow barley when the sloe is white.

Sow seeds in the afternoon when the earth is drawing in; and don't water newly set plants too late in the day – 'they don't like to be shivering in their shoes' as my gardener tells me.

## Superstitions

Planting seed can be a wasteful and expensive business when animals think that we are providing their meals: the son of a Lincolnshire gardener quoted his father's sayings:

*Four seeds in a hole:*
*One for the rook, one for the crow,*
*One to rot and one to grow*

or

*One for the birds*
*One for the mice*
*Two for the master*

Thomas Hyll, the 16th-century English gardener, suggests mixing seeds with soot before planting them: this protects them from birds and other predators and is surely worth a try to avoid disappointment.

**A fruit crop's success may depend on grafting the tree during a full or waxing moon.**

# Planting Calendar

The food-for-free season starts in spring with blossoms and young leaves and the spring crop of mushrooms. Throughout the summer you can pick a wide range of greens, herbs and flowers with which to make salads, cordials, pies and ice-creams. Come the autumn the harvest becomes a serious business with the plentiful annual yields of berries, nuts, mushrooms and fruits that cloak the autumn hedgerows and fields. This calendar is a general guide to how you can make the most of the wild harvest by freezing or storing seasonal foods. It also gives advice on which plants are available at which times of the year.

## Spring

alexanders

birch

bistort

chickweed

comfrey

corn salad

crab-apple blossom

dandelion

garlic mustard

hawthorn blossom

mushrooms

nettles

violets

wild garlic

## For the Freezer

soups, quiches and pies, tarts, ice-creams, cakes and cookies, sauces, sorbets, gratins

## For the larder

jams, jellies, chutneys, ketchups, wines, cheeses and butters, pickles, curds, syrups, relishes

## For the Storecupboard

cordials, preserves in brandy, vinegars, teas and tisanes, dried mushrooms

## Summary

## Summer

angelica
bittercress
borage
camomile
chives
clary
comfrey
corn salad
deadnettle
fat hen
elderflowers
good King
Henry
lady's mantle
lime
mallow
marigold
marjoram
marsh samphire
meadowsweet

mint
nasturtium
nettle
plantain
purslane
rose petals
salad burnet
seakale
sorrel
sow thistle
tansy
thyme
watercress
wild raspberry
wild strawberry
yarrow

## Autumn

bilberry
blackberry
bullace
cherry
chestnut
cloudberry
cobnut
crab-apple
cranberry

dewberry
elderberry
juniper
medlar
mushroom
rowan
sloe
walnut
winter cress

# SOIL

A gardener friend with a propensity to poetry tells me that adding chemicals to the soil makes it deaf to the music of the spheres. She is convinced that they are toxic and the effects detrimental. She inherited a famous garden in Hertfordshire and has worked to maintain the stunning planting. Paths meander through great mature trees, and beautiful shrubs make a backdrop for herbaceous flowering plants in spring and summer. As you wander you come across a pond, a summer house, a spinney, and everywhere is designed for a vista. Her mother-in-law told her how to get rid of weeds on the many paved areas: to sprinkle salt between the cracks. She also uses salt on the asparagus bed after it dies back, to keep the weeds down. Practical experience, hard work, and using much traditional country wisdom have contributed to the creation of work of art.

An American acquaintance takes cabbage leaves and makes them into a mush with water in the blender and pours this in the cracks along her paths or over the flower beds to prevent weeds germinating in springtime.

Soil needs nourishment, but it gets it from humus – organic matter from decomposing plant and animal remains – as well as compost. So allow stinging nettles in your garden – they stimulate the formation of humus, the blackish-brown soil that you can see around a patch of nettles. You can also use seaweed extract as a soil conditioner. And use natural, renewable boosters such as bone meal, shredded bark, well-rotted manure and green manure.

**A good rich compost with plenty of humus worked in will enrich the soil.**

# THE NATURAL GARDEN

Soil needs trace elements to enable plants to absorb valuable minerals in the soil. Nitrogen is released into the soil by growing legumes, and clovers are the best fixers, along with blue lupin, alfalfa, peas, fenugreek and beans. Tobacco plants and tansy both accumulate potassium. Crushed egg shells can be added to contribute calcium. Soils with a high level of organic matter and nitrogen tend to have lower levels of fungal decay because they produce more ethylene.

Help to prevent erosion by using mulches; use lawn mowings, shred up leaves and pine needles. Strawberries love the acidity of a pine needle mulch. Leaf litter protects the topsoil and is an invaluable soil food, providing minerals and by-products which feed the microlife of the soil and indirectly the plants themselves. Microlife enhancement means enrichment: keep the ground covered with weeds in winter and the worms will turn the soil for you underneath: this is ancient wisdom. In addition, growing yarrow and valerian encourages worms and other creatures. Add some soot to the soil to enrich it and break it up. If your soil is very alkaline give it plenty of moisture and organic material.

Weeds are not necessarily always an evil: there are positive ways of looking at this much-maligned inhabitant of the garden, which has an advocate in the poet Ralph Waldo Emerson: 'What is a weed?' he declaims. Answer: 'A plant whose virtues have not yet been discovered'. Some weeds are valuable mineral accumulators and enrich the soil: weeds in the garden are rich in the particular minerals that the soil may lack. By the law of return they feed the soil population which in its cycle builds up fertility: insect remains are of special value because the 'chitin' which forms the body armour is believed to improve plants' disease resistance.

Other weeds aerate the soil and help with drainage: for example dandelion and coltsfoot break up heavy clay. Some are capable of lessening the impact of heavy rain on the ground. They provide shelter and food for small animals whose excreta help fertilise the soil. Hoeing weeds and allowing them to remain *in situ* helps to conserve moisture, as well as releasing nutrients into the soil as they decompose.

# COMPOST

The art of composting is also a science, one which my friend Barbara, who is both plantswoman and gardener, has perfected. A stream runs through her beautiful garden, which is bordered by a cowslip meadow. The vegetable garden, edged with a young yew hedge, is next to a formal garden full of old-fashioned roses. Her knowledge and understanding about how plants and soils work are the foundations of this exceptional garden. Set behind a wild-flower area in one corner of the land is a row of compost bins all neatly cared for and surrounded by comfrey plants to layer in with the garden and household waste. Composting is an art-form here: she dismisses the over-use of artificial fertilisers since it doesn't give the soil the structure it needs, and she feels that you can over-feed with chemicals and upset the balance of nature. If you work with rotted compost, nature does it for you, and she just forks it into the topsoil at the rate of one bucket per square metre/yard. The Chinese use manure-based hot-beds to warm the soil so that they can grow vegetables all the year round.

Barbara separates herbaceous waste, weeds and household waste from grass clippings, leaves are kept to rot separately, and tired topsoil, long grass, other bits and pieces are mixed with farmyard manure, which provides phosphates, potash and nitrogen as well as humus. This is turned regularly with a long-handled hay-fork.

Of her 14 compost bins, four are for household waste, four for grass clippings (in netting cages to allow air), two for leaves (best chopped by the mower, rather than left whole) and four for miscellaneous bits and pieces. 'There is nothing like compost', she declares, 'it is so rich in nutrients. Everything you take from the ground you have to put back. Everything natural can return to be recycled.' She uses farmyard manure more for its fibre than for the nutrients – roots need air and moisture so dig it in for an ideal growing medium. It makes a beautiful loam.

It is no surprise, says Barbara, that allotments are proverbially so fertile: she observes that they have no public toilets so a certain amount of 'recycled cider' returns to the soil. Slurry from sewage farms goes on to farmland, and rightly so. The idea of throwing it away into the sea or rivers is sacrilege to her. In her garden the walnut tree stands above their septic tank and it is a huge and healthy tree with lustrous leaves and abundant fruit. The grass in the meadow, above the weeper system from the house, is lush and verdant. 'The answer lies in the soil' indeed.

Compost makes quicker in the warm weather (roughly three months) than in colder months, when it will take up to twice as long. Air circulating in the compost heap is essential. Mix grass cuttings with other materials to prevent them forming a airtight 'mat'.

It is wise to keep the compost heap as far away from the vegetable patch as possible because those bugs that help the compost decay are not always the ones you want around your cabbages – the slugs, snails and earwigs, for example! Don't place your compost heap under conifers – their turpentine substances retard fermentation. Never start compost on grass – remove the sods first since they also delay fermentation. Birch and elder trees seem to have a beneficial effect on compost bins placed nearby.

**Seaweed products release trace elements back into the soil and make a gentle fertiliser.**

# COMPOST PLANTS

Most annual weeds (except ones which have seeded) can go on the compost heap – they contain valuable minerals which return to the soil and replenish it. Exceptions are perennial weeds such as couch grass, ground elder and bindweed which will only multiply in the compost. And don't put on any weed seeds as they will simply remain dormant until the compost is used. Some of the best compost plants include alfalfa, dandelion, bark of oak, camomile, valerian, comfrey, spinach, sunflowers, yarrow, and as many herbs as possible (except wormwood). Yarrow is a fast activator of compost.

Don't however put woody or thorny material on to the heap as it doesn't decompose – especially roses which may harbour mildew or black spot. Conifers and other evergreens don't break down easily either. Don't put earthy roots on the compost heap: the earth will lower the temperature, and the roots of brussels sprouts and greens may cause fungus problems. Potato tops may carry blight, so it is better to burn them. Potato peelings should be treated against sprouting before being added to the compost heap.

Nettles make an excellent addition to the compost heap because they are so rich in minerals, they help fermentation and are an excellent soil builder. Barbara layers them in between other waste, including bonfire ash which provides iron, and she recommends lots of thin layers in the bin. You can use the friable humus around nettle patches as straight compost.

Comfrey is rich in potash, nitrogen and phosphates, so you can lay the wilted leaves on the soil as compost, particularly between rows of potatoes and around tomato plants in the greenhouse. Or put in layers between other compost: Barbara grows comfrey next to the bins so it is always handy. You can also make an excellent liquid manure from comfrey in the same way as nettles (see below).

**Let nettles grow in wild patches: humus forms and, dug in, will enrich the soil.**

Seaweed products release trace elements slowly back into the soil and make a gentle fertiliser. They help resistance to disease and stimulate micro-life in the soil.

Liquid nettle manure poured on to the soil will promote plant growth and protect plants against unhealthy conditions. Cut the nettles and cover them with water. Allow to decompose for three weeks. This liquid can also be used as a spray for foliar feed.

Or soak a sack of horse compost in 15 litres/4 gallons of water overnight, a Herefordshire gardener told me, and use the liquid to enrich the soil. Human or animal hair – the hair from your brush or the molted coat of your dog – can be added to the heap, as they are full of trace minerals.

A gardener who opens her garden to the public told me that she digs in bits of old carpet and bolsters which rot away and enrich the soil. Even old boots will do, she tells me. Her annual herbaceous display of flowers and shrubs is heavenly. She gives her onions a top-dressing of soot during the growing season, and her magnificent lilies are nourished with wood ash. Her delphiniums, hollyhocks and sunflowers all benefit from fortnightly liquid lunches of beer, and her leeks love Guinness! Slightly milky water is also a good manure for herbaceous plants.

An Indian friend with green fingers mulches her roses with all the tea-leaves from the household, and sometimes crushed eggshells. Her mother swears by bananas: the skins are a rich source of magnesium, sulphur, silica and sodium, trace elements which ensure a magnificent show of flowers. She layers them just under the surface of the soil. I know several gardeners who water their roses with tea and claim that this increases their scent and encourages healthy growth.

**Roses are greedy feeders at the best of times.**

# Companion Planting

Some of the great successes of gardening lore are to be found in the realm of companion planting. In Bulgaria, where vast quantities of roses are grown commercially for attar and rose oil, they are grown alongside onion and garlic crops. It has been shown that inter-cropping roses with garlic produces a far stronger perfume in the rose, an effect you can also get by fertilising your rose bush with compost made from garlic and onion refuse. All the alliums have fungicidal properties and attract beneficial insects, and greenfly detest garlic.

Companion planting has been practised since the Roman times. Gardeners who are observant over the years notice that some plants have a beneficial effect on each other and others grown together seem to do badly. Companion planting works in various ways. Some plants provide shelter from wind and sun, others give off root and leaf secretions which affect their neighbours either beneficially or adversely. Some plants may improve the soil by accumulating minerals, or by providing green manure or humus. Some may repel harmful insects and other pests, or act as decoys, or they may support insect populations which are beneficial to neighbouring plants. Or they may attract birds which prey on these pests.

Some plants are found to reduce the amount of fungal and other diseases in nearby plants, due to their chemical secretions.

Growing sweet peas up sunflowers is a good example of this kind of symbiosis: the legumes, of which sweet peas are one, release nitrogen into the soil. In turn, in this case, the sunflowers provide support and shelter. There is a particularly symbiotic relationship between the potato and horseradish.

**Foxgloves are good companions for most plants, since they store iron, calcium, silica, manganese and potassium in their leaves, which then drop to act as green manure.**

But there are examples of bad companions too: basil hates rue, tomatoes dislike fennel and kohlrabi, the brassicas and tomatoes don't grow well together. Roses dislike boxwood. Garlic, onions and shallots inhibit the growth of beans and peas, and pumpkins dislike potatoes. Never grow raspberries with blackberries, or radishes with hyssop. Tomatoes near potatoes have stunted growth, and the potato loses resistance to blight. Cabbages don't like the proximity of strawberries or early potatoes. And bad combinations will produce more problems with pests and mineral shortages.

# Good Companions

**Alliums** are strongly scented and discourage pests from attacking nearby plants. Since they also accumulate sulphur, they have a fungicidal effect. They are particularly beneficial for carrots, tomatoes and lettuces.

**Asparagus** and tomatoes make excellent companions because root secretions from the asparagus kills trichodorus, a nematode that attacks tomato roots. In turn, the tomato guards against asparagus beetle. Parsley also protects against this beetle, so this trio will thrive together.

**Beans**, especially broad beans, and potatoes grow well together, and potatoes repel the bean beetle: the beans release nitrogen into the soil which helps the potatoes, greedy nitrogen feeders. All leguminous species fix nitrogen in the soil which helps not only potatoes but also carrots, cauliflowers, beets, cucumbers and cabbages. Runner beans and celery grown close together help each other. Blackfly can be prevented if broad beans are planted near dill.

**Cabbages** thrive near aromatic herbs, whose leaf and root exudations deter pests. This is especially true of mint and sage which repel the white cabbage butterfly. Tomatoes and celery help cabbages in a similar way, by deterring the cabbage white from laying its eggs on the vegetables. Dill, chamomile, golden rod and late potatoes have all been noticed to have beneficial effect on cabbages.

**Carrots** will not suffer from carrot root fly if the rows are interplanted with any of the allium family – chives, spring onions or Welsh onions.

**Some of gardening's greatest successes come with the use of companion planting.**

**Cauliflowers** grow well with peas, onions, potatoes and celery. Celery deters the cabbage white butterfly, and celery and leeks grown together attract many beneficial insects especially predatory wasps.

**Chives**, one of the allium family, keep fungal diseases down, and next to carrots, help them grow tasty. The carrot root fly will be kept at bay. Chives discourage blackspot on roses, scab on apples and guard against aphids on tomatoes.

39

**Chamomile accumulates potassium and sulphur and is a host to hoverflies and wasps**

**Chamomile** grown next to peppermint makes both plants produce more essential oil. Chamomile accumulates potassium and sulphur and is a host to hoverflies and wasps, so grown next to cabbage and onions improves them in both yield and flavour.

Chamomile's beneficial health-giving presence is well known to country folk who have nicknamed it the 'plant doctor' because introduced near sick specimens it helps them recover.

Aromatic herbs in general help plants growing around them, since their root and/or leaf exudations make them distasteful to pests. You see few weeds around rosemary, rue and wormwood because these plants inhibit the germination of seeds. The secretions of wormwood are so strong that nothing thrives nearby, so it needs to be grown in isolation.

**Foxgloves** have a benign influence on most plants, stimulating their growth by accumulating potassium, iron and calcium, silica and manganese to high levels in their leaves, which then drop and act as green manure to the soil around. They are especially good with pine trees.

**Lettuces** are good companions with chervil and dill since the herbs act as a decoy to aphids and other predatory insects.

**Limnanthes douglasii**, a famous bee plant, is excellent next to shrubs and soft fruit. It attracts pollinators as well as predators such as hoverflies. Insect remains and by-products add nutrients to the soil.

**Mexican or African marigolds** (*Tagetes sp.*) have a root secretion which kills minute parasitic worms known as nematodes. Grown near the greenhouse, they will keep whitefly off tomato plants, since the odour of leaves and blossoms acts as an insect repellent. They also attract predatory hoverflies. They are excellent underplanted in the rose beds, keeping pests off the bushes.

**Nasturtiums** secrete root and leaf exudations which make them distasteful to pests. They help to keep whitefly from the greenhouse, aphids from broccoli and woolly aphids from the apple trees. Radishes thrive near nasturtiums.

**Nettles** (deadnettles, *Lamium sp.*) produce nectar for early bees and other insects, and are beneficial to vegetables. They may also deter the potato bug. When grown next to peppermint the production of the herb's essential oil is increased considerably. They help the ripening of tomatoes.

**Onions** repel carrot fly and carrots repel onion fly, so grown in alternate rows both thrive; the respective flies get confused! Onions go well with brassicas, tomatoes and lettuces since the strong smell keeps off pests. Sited next to strawberries they prevent mould on the fruit. Onions can be protected from onion fly, which is repelled by chamomile planted close by.

**Peas**, with their leguminous gift of fixing nitrogen in the soil, thrive next to radishes and all root crops, and radishes and chervil like each other.

**Potatoes** like the proximity of sweetcorn, and all squashes, including pumpkin, thrive with corn, an early discovery of the North American Indians. Sunflowers grown around the edges of the potato beds are found throughout Croatia and Poland, both growing larger when combined. Peas provide nitrogen in the soil, and potatoes are greedy nitrogen feeders.

**Roses** underplanted with lavender will not suffer from aphid attacks, and chives also have the same effect, and make the roses more fragrant.

**Runner beans** and sweetcorn thrive together since the beans release nitrogen back into the soil which the corn uses, and the beans use the corn to climb up. Sweetcorn, peas and brassicas make a good trio.

**Salsify** helps leeks and carrots, repelling the carrot root fly.

**Spinach** and strawberries love each other. Spinach adds saponins to the soil, which binds the humus together with coarser materials, helping it to retain moisture.

**Strawberries** combine well with runner beans and borage, both liking the same minerals in the ground. The strawberries help to ward off brown spot on the beans. Pine needles mulches on strawberries are particularly beneficial.

**Sweetcorn** planted with dill make both plants grown larger.

**Tomatoes** prevent gooseberries being attacked by their usual pests. They thrive near nettles and parsley, which stimulates their growth. Mexican or African marigolds help to prevent tomato eel-worm.

**Yarrow** helps all the aromatic herbs and is beneficial to all vegetables; a border of yarrow around the vegetable plot makes for a healthy harvest. It attracts worms and other creatures whose remains are of special value to soil life – chitin from their body armour is believed to help the plants' resistance to disease.

**Roses underplanted with lavender will not suffer from aphid attacks, and chives also have the same effect, and make the roses more fragrant.**

**Gourds, like all members of the marrow family, are best grown apart from potatoes.**

# BAD COMPANIONS

**Beans** will have a poorly developed crop if grown near gladioli. The growth of runner beans will be poor if interplanted with fennel.

**Cauliflower** should not be planted into soil where a crop of spinach has previously been grown.

**Strawberries** dislike cabbage plants and will not crop well when grown in proximity.

**Dill** grown near carrots will hinder good strong roots developing.

The leaves of **Walnut** trees should not be composted as they inhibit the growth of most things.

**Sunflowers** should not be grown near potatoes.

Do not grow **Roses** near box hedges; they may look pretty but the roots will get tangled and neither will do well.

Chemicals left in the ground by **cabbages** are disliked by radishes, so choose another patch of ground to sow radishes. This works the other way around too.

Members of the **Marrow** family are best grown apart from potatoes.

# BIRDS IN THE GARDEN

Although generally birds attract a bad press when it comes to the garden, most of them, barring pigeons, actually keep insects and pests down more than they destroy crops. Bulfinches have been known to strip a plum or cherry tree of buds, but mostly they do so for the sap and succulence of fresh shoots and, providing there's plenty of water around the place, they will leave shoots untouched.

Birds are useful in fertilising plants, as well as eating aphids, harmful insects and many of the seeds of common weeds.

Preventing birds attacking crops is a perennial problem. Loganberries are so prickly that birds find them hard to attack, unless there is a little space on which to land and gobble. Fruit cage produce is particularly beloved by birds and you little realise how much they can munch until visiting the red currant bushes, once laden and now stripped clean. through a hole in the netting. Cherries disappear with enormous speed unless netted. Pigeons love brassicas and can destroy a small row of young plants in no time at all. Lettuces too are attractive. Yet the friendly sparrow is disappearing fast.

During harsh winters make a birdcake from 6 tablespoons of stale brown breadcrumbs stirred into 6 tablespoons of melted fat; stir and set in the fridge in a small glass bowl. Turn out and put on a bird table where cats and other attackers cannot reach the goodies, so that birds may feed freely in cold, frosty weather. Nuthatches, all the blue tits, coal tits, great tits and robins in the world will come to feed.

Earthworms improve the soil by aerating it; to attract them, pick valerian leaves and cover with boiling water.

# A MISCELLANY OF LORE

It is said in the North of England that rabbits are supposed to dislike onions; Peter Rabbit does not deal with this issue! A row around the outside of the vegetable patch may be beneficial.

Wormwood is avoided by slugs and snails; plant it near to your hostas and the leaves stand a better chance of surviving through the summer months when snails seem to find these leaves a great source of pleasure.

Moles hate the roots of euphorbias (milk spurge), and can be moved out of the garden by sinking empty wine bottles into the ground; the noise of the wind frightens them when they are digging underground. They can dig their tunnels at the rate of 20cm/8in a minute but they eat the larvae of caterpillars and other insects that live just on or above the soil. Another plant the mole is said to dislike is the elder; I have never seen a mole heap under one.

Earthworms improve the soil by aerating it; to attract them, pick valerian leaves and cover with boiling water. Dilute the extract when cooled in the proportions of one to four and put into a container with a top; shake thoroughly and pour directly onto the soil.

Wood-ash and water mixed to a paste is said to repel deer eating the bark of fruit trees in extremely cold weather. Deer also hate the smell of hops so growing these around the perimeter fencing may help ward off deer marching around and nipping off buds, only to toss them to the ground.

Hang herbs such as lavender and rosemary amongst the roses and the deer will keep away. Hang wormwood in tree seedlings; their bitterness is said to repel deer.

Spread garden lime over lawns in early spring on a dry day; this helps to sweeten the soil and prevents dandelion seeds germinating in the grass. When it next rains, the lime will be washed in.

# Good Plants and Garden Flower Lore

*More in the garden grows*
*Than the gardener sows*
*Spanish Proverb*

The earliest known medicines and antiseptics came from herbs and flowering plants, and before their properties were understood scientifically they were believed to be magic. Much fascinating country lore accumulated over the ages, some based on their practical virtues, some imbued with superstition. Flower and tree lore is an enchanting combination of the two.

Pick and choose between the plants listed below. Encourage what grows naturally in your soil, particularly if the flowers are pretty and the plant does not get out of control and rampage at the expense of all others.

There are good weeds and bad weeds. Poppies, forget-me-nots and celandines have all been thought of as weeds – taking over the plot when not required in such profusion – but have grace and charm when controlled. Those such as ground elder and bindweed appear to pop out of the ground everywhere and, unless dug out so that every single piece of root is removed, they can take over completely, because every little piece of root left in the ground just becomes a new plant. But many weeds have high levels of nutrient rich chemicals, which can be utilised to make fungicides and the like.

**Yarrow** (*Achillea*) is *herbe aux charpentiers* because it healed instantly wounds made by carpenters' tools. Achilles was said to have cured his warriors' wounds with its leaves, hence its botanical name *Achillea millefolium*.

Today it is still used as a homeopathic medicine. An infusion can be used to detox and is very calming, but it should not be taken by pregnant women.

> *'Yarrow away, Yarrow away, bear a white blow?*
> *If my lover loves me, my nose will bleed now.'*

This saying shows the love aspect of yarrow; it is also said that the Irish hang up yarrow in their houses to ward off sickness on the Eve of St John.

Grow the pretty *Achillea 'Coronation Gold'* for the best show of yellow flowers or the more common species, *Achillea millefolium*, with its white flowerheads tinged with pink. It self-seeds.

**Box** sprigs were often placed at the door of a house at which there was a funeral. Each of the mourners would pick one up and later drop it into the open grave. Box was often used in well-dressing.

The leaves of box were used to make a hair dye and perfume from the bark. Boxwood is well loved by furniture makers because it does not warp and was used to make religious plates, musical instruments and for carvings; it still is today. In America in particular, box is grown as a hedging plant to break winds coming across the plains. Grow *Buxus sempervirens* (common box) or the dwarf variety if you have little room – *Buxus sempervirens* 'Suffruticosa'. There is a pretty variegated version, *Buxus sempervirens* 'Elegantissima'.

**Marigold** (*Calendula officinalis*) is a symbol of constancy in love, and a flower of the sun. A conserve or tea will allay depression, and a flower head rubbed onto a wasp or bee sting is an instant cure. Thunder may follow if you pick marigolds. Boiling the flowers produces a yellow dye, and the petals can be used in salad (see below). The volatile oil is a wound-healer. A hardy annual, these cheerful flowers need sun to look their best, and open flowers are said to forecast a day when there'll be no rain.

Plant French marigolds (*tagetes*) at the entrance of the greenhouse and they are said to ward off infestations of white fly and other aphids.

## Marigold Petal Salad

At the height of summer when marigolds run around the garden there are plenty to spare for the table. Combine the petals with some nasturtium leaves and you have a deliciously unusual salad.

### Serves 2–3

*1 oak leaf lettuce, washed and spun dry*
*1 handful nasturtium leaves, washed and shredded roughly*
*6 –8 cherry tomatoes, halved*
*50g/2oz toasted sunflower seeds*
*1 handful marigold petals*

### For the dressing

*2 tablespoons olive oil*
*2 tablespoons raspberry vinegar*
*1 tablespoons soy sauce*

Combine all the salad ingredients, reserving a scattering of marigold petals for the top. Mix the dressing ingredients together and toss thoroughly. Garnish with the remaining petals, and it is ready to serve.

**Cornflowers** (*Centaurea cyanus*) were reputed to blunt the blade of a reapers' sickle, and were once used as an ingredient of ink. Watercolourists still use the juice from the flowers, mixed with alum. A courting man could divine his love life: he put a cornflower in his pocket and only if it lived would he marry his current girlfriend.

One of the best cut flowers, nothing is more beautiful than a huge jug of these pure blue heads, and they last for a long time. The single form is more natural than the double one.

**Carnations** (*Dianthus*) have been cultivated for over two thousand years and their heavy scent was used in Elizabethan times to replace cloves, expensive spices brought in from the East. To wear a carnation meant that the wearer was betrothed and other suitors might as well give up their pursuit.

Growing border carnations and pinks is easy and they make pretty mounds of colour in the summer, particularly suitable at the front of the border. The flowers are often well-scented. Try *Dianthus caryophyllus* and *Dianthus deltoides*.

**Aconite** (*Eranthis hyemalis*) These enchanting little yellow flowers poke their heads through in the early, early springtime, a green frilly wreath of leaves and the yellow centre opening out in brassy colour when there is little else about in the garden. Plant in autumn. They look particularly good against a grassy bank. Try an alternative of *Eranthis* cilicia.

A Norwegian friend tells the story of Frigga, goddess of married love, who hid the souls of dead children in **Strawberries** (*Fragaria*) to smuggle them into Paradise. Strawberries are dedicated to the Virgin Mary.

**The unique blue of cornflowers was once used as an ingredient of ink.**

# GOOD PLANTS AND GARDEN FLOWER LORE

The **Quince** is a symbol of love and trees were dedicated in ancient times to the Goddess of Love. To dream of quinces means you will be cured of any sickness. The pulp from quince was used to make what we now call marmalade (with citrus fruits) by the Portuguese.

The *Cydonia vulgaris* trees grow to around 6m/20ft and are self-fertile. The pink flowers are extremely delicate and decorative. The fruits have a wonderful scent and are slightly furry outside; they can be mixed with apples or cooked with game to make a flavourful sauce.

**Snowdrops** (*Galanthus*) are a symbol of hope and purity, yet in some places thought unlucky in the house as the flowers are white. A single snowdrop is an omen of death.

Plant snowdrops in clumps and establish them when in foliage, 'in the green', dividing as necessary and when more are required. The bulbs of single forms of snowdrop, *'Galanthus' nivalis*, have larger flowers than do those of the double forms such as *Galanthus 'Dionysus'* or the picturesquely called *Galanthus 'Blewberry Tart'*, where the petals are tightly packed.

**Lily** (*Lilium*) symbol of virginity, purity and innocence, is a favourite flower at weddings and funerals. The madonna lily will only grow for a good woman, or where the mistress is master. A ninety-year-old woman who spent some years in the Belgian Congo in her youth and had some hair-raising experiences in the jungle, told me that the pygmies wore flame lilies in their belts to save themselves being eaten by lions!

When the first **Mulberry** leaves appear there will be no more frosts. It was a sacred tree in ancient Rome – and Burma! It was the Emperor Justinian who popularised

**Snowdrops (Galanthus) are a symbol of hope and purity, yet in some places considered unlucky in the house because white flowers are thought to invite disaster.**

them so that silk could be produced at the ends of his empire. In China the mulberry is a symbol of industry, used to feed silk worms.

*Morus alba* (the white form) and *Morus nigra* (the black form) are exceptionally long lived trees. The fruits of the black form are large-ish and dark, dark red when ripe; their juice stains everything it touches, though no known dye has been made from it. Fruits of the white form are pinkish or red but not of such good eating quality, but better as fodder for silkworms. The tree trunks can be used to make furniture, so this is a versatile tree if ever there was one!

**Forget-me-not** (*Myosotis*) was useful against dog and snake bites! Steel tempered with its juice was said to be hard enough to cut stone. Give a forget-me-not to someone starting a journey on February 29th.

**Daffodils** (*Narcissus*) – the Welsh say that whoever finds the first flower will have more gold than silver in the coming year. To point at a daffodil may stop it flowering.

**The 'Pheasant eye' narcissus smells just wonderful.**

A good **Cherry** (*Prunus avium*) crop brings good fortune: 'a cherry year a merry year' goes the old Kent saying. A friend of the family who lived in Switzerland for many years says that traditionally a new mother eats the first cherries to ensure a good crop for the rest of the season.

A useful tree in many ways, eat the fruit if picked before the birds get there and use the wood to make beautiful warm-coloured tables; the French 19th century country furniture is often found in our shops today. It is said that, grown close to potatoes, the potatoes become prone to blight. Wheat crops become poor if there's a cherry next door.

Grow varieties of *Prunus avium* such as 'Sunburst' and 'Stella' which are self-fertile and not dependent on other trees around for a good crop. The hugely showy blossom of the cherry should not be forgotton; this really is one of the most ornamental trees around and it grows to 10m/30ft high, so can be included in many a small garden.

**Celandine** (*Ranunculus ficaria*) was used as a cure for jaundice – by sympathetic magic because of its bright yellow colour. I have a friend in Suffolk who uses it on warts – and with success, and a grandmother in Oxford has done so for years. Just drop the fresh juice from the stem on to the wart and let it dry. Continue the treatment until it disappears. An alternative name for this plant is Pilewort, and the squashed roots, when mixed with wine or urine, were used as a cure for piles. Bees and flies love celandines.

These 'weeds' just arrive in the garden and look after themselves until they become a nuisance. There are double- and single-flowered species and they make good ground cover around ponds and in shaded places where it is often difficult to establish other, less vigorous plants. Their cheerful yellow faces make a spring morning of dappled sunlight quite enchanting.

**Broom** (*Sarothamnus scoparius*) has both sinister and beneficial qualities: a besom of blossoming broom would 'sweep the head of the house away', whereas the plant was a symbol of good luck and plenty and made its appearance at country weddings, tied with ribbons. Broom supplies good sources of nitrogen to the soil. Deer love nibbling the shoots in winter so beware!

Plant a **Yew** (*Taxus*) tree at the south-west corner of the house for protection. Yew is the tree of immortality, being a long-lived evergreen. The reason however that it is planted in churchyards is because all parts of the tree are poisonous: the volatile oil taxine can cause immediate death to children, cattle and sheep, and must therefore be kept inaccessible to them. The alkaloid taxol is also an important constituent in an anti-cancer drug, and you can offer your yew clippings as raw material for its processing, to firms who advertise collection from your garden.

*Taxus baccata* 'Elegantissima' is a yew to look out for. Slow growing but ultimately needing a very large space, the shoots of the new growth are bright yellow in sprintime and make a magnificent sight. Plant in a soggy patch and it will act as a draining agent, hence many yews are sited near old wells.

**Lilac** (*Syringa*) is unlucky in the house, especially white lilac (as with many white flowers). It is associated with death and it is unlucky to find a five-petalled lilac blossom.

Coming in all shades from dark reddy purple, through mauves and pinks to lilac colour and then on to whites, and in double and single forms, there are usually four petals to each flower. On average the lilac grows to around 4m/12ft high. Some varieties are more fragrant than others.

**Periwinkle** (*Vinca sp.*) has long been thought to be a magical plant, and now the Madagascan periwinkle (*Vinca rosea*) is an important medicinal source of anti-leukaemic drugs.

**Violets** (*Viola odorata*) if they bloom early it means death or an epidemic, but to dream of violets brings good fortune. Worn around the neck they prevent drunkenness. I found a "violet reviver' in a book of Grandmothers Recipes of 1901, which claimed that boiling violet leaves in water was a cure for cancer.

Violet

# HERBAL WISDOM

The art of using herbs to cure all manner of ailments goes back to the beginnings of civilisation when man was intricately connected to the natural world in his everyday life, and in tune with the cycles and rhythms of the turning year. He would observe how animals would select certain leaves to cure themselves, and how sick people would instinctively eat particular plant foods. The Bedouin mother would wash her newborn child in camel's urine: today's biologists have found this to be a protection from several sorts of infection. In the days before penicillin the Canadian lumberjack knew that the mould of bad bread was the best thing for an axe wound. Over the centuries a vast international body of wisdom has accumulated, both oral and written, some of which still survives in rural parts of the world, and a great deal of which has been authenticated by scientists.

The earliest roots of herbalism come from country people, often women, living in simple rural communities and passing on their wisdom informally down the

generations. It was only later that scholars picked up on and disseminated this knowledge by means of the written word, at about the time that 'physic' gardens came into their own. There is fragmentary evidence of ancient Egyptian 'medicinal ' gardens, which were further

**Using herbs as medicine goes back centuries to when we were more closely connected to the natural world.**

developed in Greece under the influence of Aristotle and Hippocrates, but they virtually disappeared until the Middle Ages in Europe, when herbal medicine was almost entirely practised by monks. They were the first great practising herbalists, growing 'physic herbs' in their infirmary gardens to supply the poor and the sick with medicines in the monastery hospital. Herbs were regarded as holy because they were given by God to cure our ills. The infirmary garden was small, enclosed, and sheltered, and typically would include the planting of many foreign herbs brought back by the Crusaders from Egypt and Syria. It was a peaceful place, enclosed by thick hedges or high walls: sweet-smelling and tranquil, to restore the soul as well as the body.

**During the Middle Ages herbs were grown in monastery gardens and were regarded as holy plants.**

The first formal Physic gardens were what we now know as botanical gardens. The first such in western Europe - and in the world – were set up in Pisa (1543), then Padua and Florence in 1545. Bologna, Leiden, Montpelier, Strasbourg, Uppsala, Paris, Amsterdam, Oxford and Edinburgh followed over the next 100 years. They were given the various names of – 'Hortus medicus', 'Jardin des Plantes', and 'Physick garden'. Here grew plants for medicinal, educational and scientific purposes, for students of medicine and apothecaries to use like a library.

One of the world's most famous Physic Gardens, although not the oldest, is at Chelsea, planted by the Apothecaries' Company in 1683. Linnaeus walked there, and another of its many claims to fame was that it had the first hot-house in England. Its four acres are still there to be used and enjoyed just two and a half miles from

Piccadilly Circus, for the ongoing purposes of education and science: the immense learning gleaned from this research can be found in herbals and pharmacopeia, both ancient and modern.

But healing herbs have always been a preserve of the common people too, and this wisdom has found its way into commonplace folk medicine throughout the world. Country cures have been handed down the generations because they work. They come in the diverse forms of lotions and potions, decoctions and compresses, oils and teas to heal the sick and soothe the poorly. The subject of herbs in healing is steeped in antiquity and vaster than even a comprehensive encyclopaedia. Even though only a tiny taste can be touched on here, it opens a door on a fascinating world where science meets tradition and embraces the ancient wisdom of ordinary country people.

From Babylonian times men and animals, vegetables and minerals were thought to be under the dominion of the planets. Every plant was a terrestrial star, every star a spiritualised planet. The oldest astrologers taught that the seven known planets (Sun, Moon, Mercury, Venus, Mars, Saturn and Jupiter) all had influence over plant life and that they had their own herbs, trees and flowers. Both Hippocrates and Galen advised physicians to be instructed in astronomy, and in primitive cultures worldwide the moon in particular is acknowledged as an influence in certain diseases. Many of the great herbalists have combined the profession of herbalist with astrologer. 'He must know the mathematical sciences, and especially astrologie', wrote Culpeper's contemporary, the 17th century Italian herbalist Giambattista della Porta.

*Above all things next to grammar a physician must*
*surely have his Astronomye, to know how, when and*
*at what time every medicine ought to be administered.*
16th century physician, anon

## HERBAL WISDOM

Culpeper assigned to each herb its ruling planet. The attribution of plants to the signs of the Zodiac is one of the lighter sides of astrology: the theory goes that the vibrations or force fields emitted by particular plants are compatible with and can have beneficial effects on the health of people born under the ruling of that planet.

# THE NATURAL GARDEN

**ARIES (Mars)**
thistles, nettles, brambles, mustard,
onion, peppers, geranium,
honeysuckle, witch-hazel, rosemary,
marjoram, garlic, horseradish, cowslip

**CANCER (Moon)**
water lilies and all water plants,
forget-me-nots, saxifrages, white
poppy, mouse-ear, acanthus, wild
flowers, agrimony, balm, daisies,
lettuce, cucumber

**TAURUS (Venus)**
damask roses, violets, primroses, vine,
rose, poppy, foxglove, mint, thyme,
tansy, coltsfoot, lovage

**LEO (Sun)**
sunflowers, dahlias, St. John's wort,
saffron, rue, marigold, rosemary,
borage, chamomile

**GEMINI (Mercury)**
lily of the valley, speedwell, lavender,
mild aromatic herbs (parsley, dill,
fennel, caraway, marjoram

**VIRGO (Mercury)**
lily of the valley, speedwell, lavender,
mild aromatic herbs (as Gemini),
small brightly coloured flowers,
southernwood, savory, fennel, valerian

LIBRA (Venus)

large damask roses, violets,
primroses, vine, blue flowers,
dandelion, yarrow, pennyroyal

CAPRICORN (Saturn)

pansy, henbane, hemlock, deadly
nightshade, onions, ivy, comfrey, red
beets, sorrel, Solomon's seal

SCORPIO (Mars)

thistles, nettles, brambles, onion,
mustard, peppers, dark red flowers
e.g. rhododendrons, basil, tarragon,
barberry

AQUARIUS (Uranus)

orchid, golden rain, elderberry,
fumitory, mullein, barley

SAGITTARIUS (Jupiter)

red roses (not damask),
meadowsweet, jessamine, houseleek,
asparagus, pinks, dandelion, sage,
samphire, chervil

PISCES (Jupiter and Neptune)

red roses (not damask),
meadowsweet, jessamine, houseleek,
waterlily, fig, bilberry, rose hip,
lungwort

# Herbs

The most famous of our garden herbs merit infinitely more space than is possible to give them in this book, yet it is impossible to exclude them. The great herbals of the past describe how soothing lavender is relaxant and restorative, rosemary is antiseptic and antibacterial, peppermint is a heart tonic and stomach-soother, dill and fennel water relieve colic in babies, parsley builds up iron in the blood to help anaemia… and so on.

**Yarrow** (*Achillea millefolium*) For centuries this herb, which is widespread in the temperate regions of of the world, has been used to heal wounds and stem the flow of blood. During World War I soldiers carried yarrow ointment for use as a first-aid dressing on wounds and burns. Yarrow can reduce high blood pressure and is used to cool a fever. A diuretic, it is used in urinary tract problems, and mixed in an infusion with elderflower and peppermint it is excellent for colds. Don't use yarrow in pregnancy however as it stimulates the uterus, but it can regulate menstrual periods. Chew a fresh leaf to alleviate toothache. The North American Indians used yarrow to soothe the nerves and lift the spirits, as well as curing fevers and colds.

Yarrow grows to around 1m/3ft high, and has small white flowers and a mass of feathery leaves. It has creeping roots and is invasive, so beware in a small garden.

**Marigold** (*Calendula officinalis*) A Mediterranean native, the marigold is a versatile plant: both medicinal and culinary, it also yields a yellow dye and is used in cosmetic preparations. In traditional remedies it has been used for its astringent, antiseptic, anti-fungal and anti-inflammatory properties. Taken internally for menstrual disorders and digestion – St. Hildegard recommended it for intestinal and liver problems – it is also used externally for thrush, minor cuts and grazes, chilblains and ulcers. Rub a marigold flower into a bee sting. Marigold tea can help with the hot flushes of the menopause. Since the Romans it has been used to bring down fevers, It was taken seriously as a wound herb during the American Civil war and World War I: the eminent gardener Gertrude Jekyll sent crates of marigolds from her Sussex garden to the field hospitals in France where they were made up into ointment and applied to the soldiers' wounds.

Brilliant orange flowers in spring garland the bright green leaves; marigolds grow to around 60cm/2ft high and will grow in practically any soil. Plant seed in autumn, overwinter in a sheltered position and plant out in springtime.

## Chamomile

(*Chamaemelum nobile*) Chamomile, the 'plant physician' contains muscle relaxants that calm the stomach, soothe sore eyes, and are effective in menstrual disorders. Chamomile oil relieves sciatica and arthritis, and can be administered for headaches, migraine and neuralgia.

Known as Roman chamomile, it grows to 10cm/4in with a daisy-like flower in the middle of frothy green leaves. Use *Chamaemelum nobile 'Treneague'*, it does not flower but is as a lawn, (a lot of work but romantic nonetheless).

## Eucalyptus (*Eucalyptus globulus*)

Indigenous to Australia and Tasmania, infusions of eucalyptus were an aboriginal remedy for bringing down a fever, for dysentery and sores. A woman who lived in Zimbabwe used a decoction of eucalyptus leaves for colds, coughs and flu, and as a gargle for a sore throat. Traditional Chinese medicine recommends rubbing diluted eucalyptus oil into inflamed joints to relieve arthritis. It can also be used as a compress for wounds, burns – and athlete's foot. Rub it into the temples when you have a headache, or mix it with tea-tree oil, dilute in a base oil, and rub it into hands and feet as a general tonic to boost the immune system.

**Eucalyptus**

Grows to an enormous height, 40-50m/120-150ft high in the right situation; it dislikes chilly winds which can scorch the leaves and look ugly. If it likes you it will do well.

**Eyebright** (*Euphrasia rostkoviana*)
Throughout its native Europe, eyebright is still the best known herb to treat eye conditions and has been so since the days of ancient Greece. It sharpens the sight and combats infection. The dried flowering plant is used in infusion and decoction as an anti-inflammatory and astringent, and as a mild lotion it has been used in traditional country medicine to treat conjunctivitis. You can also use this as a nasal douche for catarrh and sinusitis. As a poultice, eyebright aids the healing of minor wounds.

**Meadowsweet** (*Filipendula Ulmaria*)
Classified by the eighteenth century Swedish botanist Linnaeus as Spiraea, meadowsweet gave rise to the brand name 'aspirin' because it was from its flowerbuds that salicylic acid was first discovered in 1839 and from which aspirin was later synthesized in the 1890s. Known to herbalists as the 'herbal aspirin', meadowsweet is used as a relaxant, to promote a good night's sleep; an infusion of the leaves and flowers is food for colds and flu and fevers, It soothes gastritis, and indigestion, and is the most effective plant remedy for hyperacidity. It has been successful in the easing of arthritic and rheumatic pain. Also known as 'queen of the meadow', this beautifully fragrant plant, once used to flavour mead, is native to Europe and Asia, and has naturalised in North America.

A hardy perennial, it grows to 1.25m/4ft and has a sickly green leaf and a mass of creamy white flowers in the summer. Sow in autumn for the following year's flowering.

**Lavender** (*Lavendula officinalis*). The famous fragrance of lavender is loved for its own sake but the aromatic oil has powerful remedial values too. It is strongly sedative, so a few drops in a nightime bath will facilitate restful sleep. Some hospitals are now burning lavender oils in their wards instead of administering sleeping pills. Lavender oil is anti-depressant and can be used to lesson emotional tension. Rub lavender oil into the neck and temples for a headache, or drink lavender tea made from the flowers. Used in massage oil, lavender eases muscular aches and strains and can help rheumatism.

Common or English Lavender (L. officinalis) has purple flowers on long spikes in late summer. Grow lavenders from cuttings preferably in sunny, well drained soil in an open situation. Some varieties are not that hardy.

**Marjoram** (*Origanum sp.*) A tea of *Origanum marjorana* or *Origanum vulgare* (oregano) can be taken for colds and digestive upsets. The essential oil of marjoram is used by aromatherapists to ease digestive spasms and period pains and rubbed into rheumatic joints. Recent research shows that it can prevent premature ageing of cells, and may combat free radicals which damage healthy cells.

There are many varieties of marjoram, which generally grows to 20cm/8in. These plants are easy to divide, the safest way to obtain what you want. They like well drained soil and nooks and crannies too.

**Rosemary** (*Rosmarinus officinalis*) Rosemary is antiseptic and antibacterial and is said to be anti-ageing and a memory-enhancer. It does in fact increase the flow of the blood to the brain, and has been used in a host of ailments ranging from nervousness, exhaustion and hangovers to period pains, fevers and chest infections. A drop or two of rosemary oil rubbed into the temples dispels a headache.

Look around a good nursery for the varieties to grow. There are so many, from white flowered to deep blues and mauves. The most fragrant, *R. officinalis*, grows to 1.5m/4ft and flowers in early summer and sometimes again in early autumn.

**Rosemary**

**Dock** (*Rumex crispus*) A native of Eurasia, is now widely distributed in temperate and subtropical countries as a weed. Its long taproot extracts iron from the soil and makes it an excellent remedy for anaemia. Crushed dock leaves are well-known to relieve nettle stings and scalds, and the North American Indians applied them to boils. People have used them on ringworm and scabies, too, with success. Less well known are its detoxifying effects: since the ancient Greeks a decoction of dock has been used to clear up skin complaints and clear digestive problems. The Chinese use it to bring down fever, and dock seeds were a traditional remedy for dysentery and diarrhoea in European folk medicine. Bitter glycosides in the root stimulate the liver and are revitalising.

Dock grows vigorously with extremely long tap roots, which are difficult to dig out of the ground completely; this is a true garden weed, but there are plenty of docks to be found in the countryside.

**Sage** (*Salvia officinalis*) 'Sage the Saviour' was one of the most valued herbs of antiquity. It is a rejuvenating tonic and a memory-herb, while its antiseptic and astringent properties make it an excellent remedy for tonsilitis, asthma, catarrh and sinusitis. It is expectorant and used in coughs. It boosts the immune system and settles the stomach and liver. It is diuretic, and its astringency reduces period cramps and heavy bleeding. It is first-rate on cuts and wounds. Use sage tea as a gargle for a sore throat.

A hardy perennial growing to 60cm/2ft, sages have surprisingly beautiful and curiously shaped flowers of brilliant blue hues, and there is even a white variety. Take cuttings or sow in springtime and pot out when the plants are well established.

**Tricolor Sage**

**Elder** (*Sambucus nigra*) The elder has been in long and continuous use ever since the days of ancient Egypt. Native to Europe, North Africa and western Asia, it was the country medicine chest since all its parts could be used, the flowers, leaves, berries, bark and root. The flowers are highly anticatarrhal, and elderflower tea, sometimes mixed with yarrow, is often used in the treatment of colds and flu, or as a gargle for sore throats. The North American Indians used it for colic and also headaches. The berries have a high vitamin C content and are a prophylactic against colds and infections. They have a laxative action and you can add them to other stewed fruits.

Grows to around 4m/12ft high, and has fragrant small white flowers in cymes throughout the summer months, then deep purple berries in early autumn, which taste quite bitter. Try *Sambucus canadensis* *'Aurea'*, the variegated form. All parts of the fresh plant, including the flowers, have been known to poison.

**Comfrey** (*Symphytum officinale*)
Knitbone, boneset and bruisewort aptly describe the uses to which comfrey has been put over the centuries. It is however undergoing a lapse in popularity after carcinogenic alkaloids were found to damage liver cells if administered in vast quantities to rats who were given nothing else to eat. It is argued by the opposition that these alkaloids are destroyed on processing the herb and are not absorbed by the human digestive system. Be that as it may, comfrey has a high protein content

(35%) and is an important animal food crop in Africa. It contains vitamin B12 unlike any other plant. Above all comfrey heals damaged tissues: it contains allantoin, a substance which stimulates the production of the connective tissue that forms bone and cartilage. Used for centuries to mend fractures and relieve sprains, comfrey is efficacious on horses too: the leaves wrapped around cracked heels heal them fast. It is a native of Europe and Asia, and has been introduced all over the world. It is an extremely vigorous plant.

*Symphytum 'Hidcote Blue'* is a pretty comfrey, growing to around 50cm/20in high with pale blue flowers in late spring and sharply pointed leaves. Will grow in semi-shade.

**Feverfew** (*Tanacetum parthenium*) Today feverfew is one of the most popular herbs for treating migraine, and is undergoing extensive scientific scrutiny: trials to date report that 70% of migraine sufferers feel an improvement in their condition after taking feverfew. Native to South Eastern Europe, and introduced elsewhere around the world, you can easily grow it in the garden with its feathery leaves and daisy-like flowers. Try chewing one or two leaves a day as a prophylactic for headaches and migraines, or make a feverfew sandwich. Do this judiciously: The leaves are very bitter and can cause mouth ulcers or skin irritation.

Grows to 1m/3ft with white daisy-type flower heads in profusion. Self-seeds readily and can be invasive, growing in walls and crannies. The double flowered feverfew has interesting flowers.

**Dandelion** (*Taraxacum officinale*) Dandelion is a powerful diuretic, and dandelion tea is excellent for cellulite, water retention and urinary infections. It detoxifies the system and is beneficial in liver problems and gall bladder infections. You can eat the young leaves in salad and their diuretic action, which eliminates uric acid from the body, is helpful in rheumatism and arthritis. For warts, apply the milky sap from the stem over a few weeks. Originating from central Asia, the dandelion is now esteemed throughout the world as a valuable medicinal plant.

The flowers are used to make a delicious country wine.

**Thyme** (*Thymus vulgaris*) Thyme is a powerful antiseptic. Struck by an extremely sore throat in Morocco I bought a large bunch from the market, made an infusion and gargled with it; I also drank it as tea and the pain disappeared. It is a panacea in folk medicine for digestion, for intestinal upsets, and for any fungal infections such as thrush; it is also good for anxiety and insomnia, urinary tract infections and gout.

**Coltsfoot**

**Coltsfoot** (*Tussilago farfara*) The flowers and leaves of coltsfoot have for centuries been smoked to ease a bronchial cough. Pliny recommended this cure as far back as the second century AD, and the Greeks called it 'cough plant'. The leaves were dried, and rolled into home-rolled cigarettes, and are today to be found in herbal tobaccos, although nowadays it is more usual to take coltsfoot in the form of an infusion. It is anti-inflammatory and relieves bronchitis, catarrh, asthma, a heavy cough and laryngitis. Although a native of Europe, north and west Asia, and North Africa, coltsfoot (named after the shape of its leaf), has also been introduced and naturalised in North America.

**Nettles** (*Urtica dioica*)  Nettles are so useful that in spite of being an ubiquitous weed , they were cultivated in Scotland, Denmark and Norway for medicinal use and as a commercial source of chlorophyll. In World War 2 they were used to dress infected wounds and speed their healing. Famous in country wisdom for being a spring tonic, you can make a delicious soup or drink nettle tea. Nettles stimulate the liver and kidneys and help the body detoxify itself. Their diuretic properties help arthritis and gout, stimulate the digestive system and are helpful in respiratory infections. The nettle is an astringent remedy for menstrual irregularity and heavy bleeding. A tincture stops the bleeding from cuts and wounds, and the powdered dried leaf can be used like snuff, and will stop nose-bleeds.

My French friend Francoise insists that if you hold your breath while walking through stinging nettles, you won't get stung. It works every time, she says.

You hardly need to cultivate nettles, since they grow so commonly in the wild.

**Violet**  (*Viola odorata*)  Violet leaves are quoted in various European herbals for chronic catarrh and bronchitis, and occasionally in the treatment of rheumatism. The British Pharmacopeia of 1983 records that sweet violet (Viola odorata) has been used both internally and externally for treating cancers. A commonplace book of 1901 suggests pouring one pint of boiling water over a handful of fresh green violet leaves, covering them and letting them stand for 12 hours. Strain, dip lint into the liquid and apply as a compress. Replace when dry or cold.  I unearthed a newspaper cutting from The Times in the early 1900s telling the story of Lady M who had serious throat cancer and was on the verge of death when a friend suggested this remedy. Within a week the external swelling had gone and the pain had ceased. Another week later the cancer had disappeared.

White or purple flowered, these cheerful-faces accompany heart-shaped leaves and grow to about 8cm/3in high. Keep them out of boggy ground and they'll thrive on banks.

# BEES & BUTTERFLIES

There are five hundred bees for every human being on earth. We depend on them for crop pollination so they are therefore intrinsic to our survival on the planet. No wonder that bees have acquired so special a status in the eyes of the country people who rear them, and who for centuries have found myriad uses for their honey and wax. They are welcome visitors to any garden, cross-pollinating as they collect nectar. One of many staggering facts about bees is that it take the nectar of one and a half million flowers to make a single jar of honey.

A lady in her eighties, a committed beekeeper in our village, told me

*A swarm in May is worth a load of hay*
*A swarm in June is worth a silver spoon*

*A swarm in July is not worth a fly*

'Telling the bees' is a tradition, claimed by all who use it:

*Marriage, birth and buryin'*
*ews across the seas,*
*All you're sad and merry in*
*You must tell the bees*

If you don't, they die themselves. Furthermore all hives must be turned or moved at the moment their dead owner's corpse left the house for burial.

## Plants for a butterfly garden

I talked to a butterfly gardener in his glass-house which was full of lantana, the prime butterfly plant which produces so much nectar. Butterflies taste with their feet, he informed me! For the garden he advised leaving a corner full of nettles for the Red Admiral to lay its eggs. His wild garden included scabious, plantain, foxgloves, mallow, cornflower and some giant Scotch thistles; ragged robin in abundance and valerian scrambling along the walls. A patch of origanum attracted hordes of meadow browns, peacocks and small tortoiseshells.

He recommended aubretia, buddleia, honesty, sedums, michaelmas daisy, sweet rocket, tobacco plant, yellow alyssum, golden rod, pinks, hyssop, lilac, honeysuckle, forget me not, and violas.

# GARDEN PESTS

There are some plants that act as natural insecticides: chives and parsley deter greenfly, onion and carrot fly. Marigolds and nasturtiums repel white, black and greenfly and wormwood repels everything. Tansy deters flies, ants, and moths. Hyssop repels blackfly, Pyrethrum controls aphids and spider mites; Euphorbia lathyrus repels moles, and onions among lettuces repel rabbits.

Planting 'plant decoys' is a smart move: whitefly loves nicotiana, aphids love basil, so use them as sacrificial plants nearby more precious ones. And encourage predators: create cover in your damp spots for toads and frogs because they are good predators of pests, and encourage ladybirds by planting Limnanthes.

You can trap slugs under inverted grapefruit shells and despatch them before they attack your plants.

## Slugs

Kate, my editor, remembers childhood when her grandmother used to invert half-grapefruit shells with little 'doors' cut into them, to entice slugs in. In they came, upon which grandmother would pick them up and crush them between her fingers. She still, according to Kate, uses this infallible technique. Kate's mother doesn't bother with the grapefruit but simply picks them up when she sees them and absent-mindedly despatches them while carrying on a conversation! If you prefer a less tactile method, kill them by sprinkling them with salt. You can protect plants with a ring of sharp gravel around the bottom: this 'hurts their feet' according to the gardening expert Hugh Johnson. My gardener friend Barbara sprinkles crushed toasted eggshells around the plants – but above all she encourages her toads to do the work for her! Encourage them in your damp patches.

A friend in the village sinks a bowl of beer into the ground: the slugs fall in and drown… happy. Slugs are repelled by a mulch of oak leaves or wood ash, and will also crawl under wooden boards where you can catch them unawares.

My mother's gardener used to strip the leaves from Brussels sprouts and lay them on the ground to distract slugs away from the leaves on the plant. He also laid prickly thistles or bracken or thorny evergreen near the affected plants to deter them. He used to swear that if you put slices of turnip down for them they would die of overeating.

## Ants

Ants are repelled by growing pennyroyal, spearmint or tansy. Many pests travel up tree trunks and you can stop them with a band of grease. Throw boiling water on the nest, says Barbara. Or petrol. A medieval gardener suggests throwing sawdust from oak planks on to the anthill. According to and anonymous source who wrote Le Menagier de Paris (1393), the ants will die or leave when next rain falls, because the sawdust retains the water.

But a Chinese friend whose father was a fruit farmer told me that, since ants eat the larvae of fruit fly, he used to make little bamboo bridges for the ants to travel from tree to tree!

## Deer

Little will keep deer out apart from erecting a very tall fence. A Norwegian solution: go to the hairdresser and get a bag of human hair, fill small muslin bags with it and scatter between your plants. Deer so dislike the smell of anything human that they will go.

THE NATURAL GARDEN

**Fly** (aphids, blackfly, whitefly etc.)

Ladybirds are one of nature's most efficient predators of fly: they particularly love Artemesia and Limnanthes so if you grow some for them you will be well rewarded. They also dislike spearmint, stinging nettles and nasturtiums, so these plants will act as deterrents. Or you can simply spray fly with soapy water.

An old Essex gardener told me of a natural —as opposed to chemical —way to get rid of the greenfly, blackfly and whitefly that plague the garden during the summer months: an infusion of rhubarb leaves, used as a spray. It works. An Australian woman's grandfather used to use this, too.

*1kg/2lb rhubarb leaves*
*cold water to cover*

Bring the rhubarb leaves to the boil in a large saucepan and simmer for 2 minutes. The leaves disintegrate quickly. Leave to cool and when cold strain off. Store in bottles, keep in a cool place and use instead of chemical sprays. You can also make an effective spray for fly by soaking nettles in rainwater for three weeks. It also kills lice and aphids.

He also told me to spray cabbages with sea water to deter caterpillars, but I have found a more whimsical remedy:

*Go into the garden at dawn on Sunday and on bare knees say three Ave Marias and three Paternosters in reverence to the Trinity, then take a cabbage or some other leaf eaten by caterpillars and put inside two or three of them, and say 'Caterpillars come with me to Mass'; then take the whole thing along to church, and before listening to the Mass let it fall. After this the caterpillars will disappear from the garden — this is not a joke, it has been proved to work and its practise is still in use.*

*Girolamo Firenzuola (16th-century Italian)*

## Mildew

My mother's gardener Mr Williams used horsetail tea to combat mildew: Take two large handfuls of horsetail, and put into a large pan with water to cover. Bring slowly to the boil and simmer very gently for 20 minutes with the lid on. Set side in a cool place for 24 hours and then strain. Dilute with two-parts water to spray.

Liquid seaweed also gets rid of mildew, and chive tea is effective against mildew on gooseberry plants.

**Eliminate mildew on plants with horsetail tea.**

## Birds, spider-mites and blight

If you scatter dried powdered garlic on the ground it stops birds eating nearby plants. Try this near your fruit bushes! Spider-mites you can deter with a spray of garlic or chilli pepper (see below). And garlic tea controls blight on potatoes and tomatoes. Simplest of all, get a predator on the job: have a cat patrol near your fruit bushes, says Barbara.

*Chilli garlic spray*
*('Spider-mites' good-bye')*

*3 hot green chillies*
*3 cloves garlic*
*3–4 teaspoons washing up liquid*
*water*

Mince the chillies and garlic finely, in a blender. Put into a bowl with the washing-up liquid and add 750 ml/1¼ pints water. Leave to stand for twenty-four hours, then strain. Add a further 300 ml/½ pint of water to dilute, then pour into a bottle with a spray nozzle.

# INDEX

aconites (*Eranthis hyemalis*) 52
alfalfa 26, 33
alliums 36, 38
ants 13, 76, 77
aphids 39, 41, 42, 45, 51, 76
apples 39, 41
ash 33, 34, 47, 77
asparagus 25, 38
astrology 62-3, 64-5

bananas 34
bark 25, 33
basil 37, 76
beans 19, 26, 37, 38, 44, 42
bees 8, 14, 41, 58, 74-5
beetles 14
beetroot 38
berries 15, 22, 23
bindweed 33, 48
birds 11, 13-14, 19, 36, 45, 79
black spot 33, 39
blackberries 37
blackfly 38, 76
blackthorn 15
blight 37, 79
bonemeal 25
borage 42
box (*Buxus*) 37, 44, 49
brassicas 37, 42, 45
broccoli 41
broom (*Sarothamnus scoparius*) 58
brown spot 42
brussels sprouts 33, 77
butterflies 8, 38, 39, 75

cabbages 25, 37, 38, 40, 44, 78
calcium 26, 37, 41
carnations (*Dianthus*) 52
carrots 19, 38, 39, 42, 44
cauliflowers 38, 39, 44
celandines (*Ranunculus ficaria*) 48, 58
celery 38, 39
chamomile 33, 38, 40-1, 42, 67
cherry (*Prunus avium*) 57
chervil 41, 42
chives 38, 39, 42, 76, 79
clovers 26
coltsfoot (*Tussilago farfara*) 13, 26, 72-3
comfrey (*Symphytum officinale*) 29, 33, 71
companion planting 7-8, 36-44
compost 8, 29-30, 33-4
conifers 30, 33
cornflowers (*Centaurea cyanus*) 52
couch grass 33
courgettes 19

cucumbers 19, 38
currants 45

daffodils (*Narcissus*) 56
dandelions (*Taraxacum officinale*) 13, 26, 33, 47, 72
deer 47, 58, 77
delphiniums 34
dill 38, 41, 43, 44
dock (*Rumex crispus*) 69-70

earwigs 30
egg shells 26, 34, 77
elder (*Sambucus nigra*) 30, 47, 70-1
ethylene 26
eucalyptus (*Eucalyptus globulus*) 67
euphorbia (milk spurge) 47, 76
eyebright (*Euphrasia rostkoviana*)68

fennel 37, 44
fenugreek 26
fertility 11, 26, 30, 34, 43
feverfew (*Tanacetum parthenium*) 71-2
flies 58
fly, see aphids
folklore 7-8, 48
forget-me-nots (*Myosotis*) 48, 56
foxgloves 47, 41
fungal infections 26, 33, 36, 39

garden pests 76-9
garlic 19, 36, 37, 79
gladioli 44
gooseberries 43, 79
grapefruit 76
grass cuttings 26, 29, 30
greenflies 36, 76
ground elder 33, 48

harvesting 11, 22
hawthorn 15
hollyhocks 34
horseradish 36
horsetail 79
hostas 47
hoverflies 40, 41
humus 25, 29, 36, 42
hyssop 37, 76

iron 33, 37, 41

kohlrabi 37

ladybirds 76, 78
lantana 75
lavender (*Lavandula officinalis*) 42, 47, 68

leaf litter 26, 29, 77
leeks 34, 39, 42
legumes 26, 36, 38
lettuces 38, 41, 42, 45, 76
lilac (*Syringa*) 59
lily (*Lilium*) 34, 55
lime 47
*Limnanthes douglasii* (poached egg plant) 41, 76, 78
loganberries 45
lupins 26

magnesium 34
manganese 37, 41
manure 25, 29, 34, 37, 41
marigolds (*Calendula officinalis*) 66-7
   marigold petal salad 51
marigolds, French, Mexican or African (*Tagetes*) 41, 43, 51, 76
marjoram (*Origanum*) 69
marrows 19, 44
meadowsweet (*Filipendula ulmaria*) 68
mildew 33, 79
minerals 26, 33, 37, 40, 41
moles 47, 76
moon 7, 8, 16-17, 18-19
mulberry (*Morus*) 55-6
mulch 26, 34, 77
mushrooms 22

nasturtiums 41, 76, 78
nematodes 38, 41, 43
nettles (*Urtica dioica*) 25, 33, 34, 41, 43, 73, 75, 78
nitrogen 26, 29, 33, 38, 41, 58
nuts 15, 22, 23

onions 19, 34, 36, 37, 38, 39, 40, 42, 47, 76

parsley 38, 43, 76
parsnips 19
peas 19, 26, 37, 39, 42
pennyroyal 77
peppermint 40, 41
periwinkle (*Vinca*) 59
phosphates 29, 33
pines 26, 41
planting 18-19
planting calendar 22-3
poppies 48
potash 29, 33
potassium 26, 37, 40, 41
potatoes 19, 33, 37, 38, 39, 41, 42, 44, 57, 79
pumpkins 37, 42
pyrethrum 76

rabbits 47, 76
radishes 37, 41, 42, 44
raspberries 37
rhubarb 78
rosemary (*Rosmarinus officinalis*) 41, 47, 69
roses 33, 34, 42, 36, 37, 39, 41, 47
rue 37, 41

sage (*Salvia officinalis*) 70
salt 25, 77
saponins 42
scab 39
seaweed 25, 30, 34, 79
seed crops 18-19
shallots 19, 37
silica 34, 37, 41
slugs 30, 76-7
snails 30, 47
snowdrops (*Galanthus*) 55
sodium 34
soil 24-35
soot 26, 34
sowing 11, 18-19, 21
spearmint 77, 78
spider-mites 76, 79
spinach 33, 42, 44
strawberries (*Fragaria*) 26, 37, 42, 44, 52
sulphur 34, 40
sunflowers 33, 34, 36, 42, 44
sweet peas 36
sweetcorn 42, 43

tansy 26, 76, 77
thistles 13
thyme (*Thymus vulgaris*) 72
tobacco plants (*Nicotiana*) 26, 76
tomatoes 33, 37, 38, 41, 42, 43, 79
trees 14, 15, 19, 30, 33, 44, 45, 47, 55-6

valerian 33, 46, 47
violets (*Viola odorata*) 59, 73

wasps 39, 40
weather 7, 8, 10
   clouds and wind 12
   cold weather 15
   fine weather 11, 17
   rain 13-15
weeds 25, 26, 29, 32, 45, 48
wheat 57
whitefly 41, 51, 76
worms 14, 26, 43, 46, 47
wormwood 33, 41, 47, 76

yarrow (*Achillea*) 33, 43, 48-9, 68
yew (*Taxus*) 58-9